536

MY WORLD OF SCIENCE

Hot and Cold

Revised and Updated

Angela Royston

Heinemann Library
Chicago, Illinois

© 2001, 2008 Heinemann Library
a division of Pearson Inc.
Chicago, Illinois

Customer Service 888-454-2279
Visit our website at www.heinemannlibrary.com

Editorial: Rebecca Rissman
Design: Joanna Hinton-Malivoire
Picture research: Melissa Allison and Mica Brancic
Production: Duncan Gilbert

Originated by Chroma Graphics (Overseas) Pte Ltd
Printed and bound in China by South China Printing Co. Ltd

12 11 10 09 08
10 9 8 7 6 5 4 3 2 1

ISBN: HB: 978-1-4329-1434-9, PB: 978-1-4329-1456-1

The Library of Congress has cataloged the first edition as follows:
Royston, Angela
Hot and cold/ Angela Royston
        p. cm.—(My world of science)
Includes bibliographical references and index
ISBN 1-58810-241-6
1.   Heat—Juvenile literature. 2. Cold—Juvenile literature. 3. Temperature measurements—Juvenile literature. [1. Heat. 2. Cold. 3. Temperature.] I. Title.
QC256. R69 2001
536-dc21
                                        00-012870

Acknowledgements
The publishers would like to thank the following for permission to reproduce photographs: © Eye Ubiquitous p. **7** (Sylvia Greenland); © Getty Images pp. **5** (Stockfood Creative), **15**; © Masterfile p. **22** (Boden/Ledingha); © Robert Harding pp. **4**, **8**; © Science Photo Library pp. **9** (Geoff Tompkinson), **14**; © Trevor Clifford pp. **6**, **10**, **11**, **12**, **13**, **16**, **17**, **19**, **20**, **21**, **23**, **24**, **25**, **26**, **27**, **28**, **29**; Trip p. **18** (H. Rogers).

Cover photograph reproduced with permission of © Masterfile (Janet Foster).

The publishers would like to thank Jon Bliss for his assistance in the preparation of this book.

Contents

Any words appearing in the text in bold, **like this**, are explained in the glossary.

Hot and Cold

Some things are hot. When food is very hot, you can see **steam** rising from it. You need to be careful not to burn your mouth when you eat it.

This baked potato is very hot.

Other things are very cold. As you lick a
frozen juice popsicle, it makes your lips
and tongue cold, too.

Danger!

Many things may be so hot they can burn and hurt you. An oven may be very hot.

People use oven gloves to help protect their hands from very hot pans.

Keep away from hot things even when they are turned off. A hot iron smoothes out creases in clothes. It stays hot for a long time after it has been turned off.

Neither Hot nor Cold

Some things are neither hot nor cold. The water in a swimming pool can be cool, warm, or **lukewarm**.

This baby's bath water is warmer than the water in a swimming pool. But it is probably cooler than your bath water.

Temperature

We use words like warm, cool, hot, and cold to talk about **temperature**. The boy in the picture is testing the temperature of the bath water with his hand.

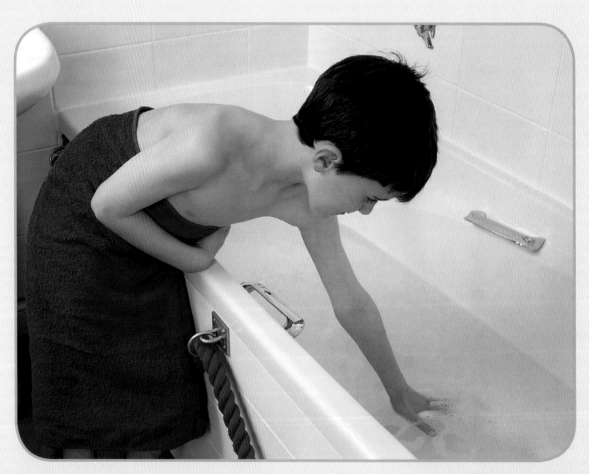

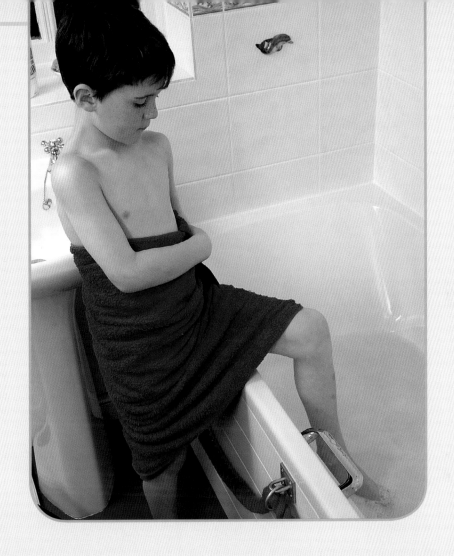

Different parts of the body feel temperature
differently. The bath water will probably feel
hotter to the boy's foot than to his hand.

Testing Temperatures

Temperatures can feel different when you are hot or cold. The girl is holding her hands in warm water. The boy is holding his hands in cold water.

warm water

cold water

lukewarm water

Now they both put their hands in
lukewarm water. The girl says it feels
cool. The boy says it feels warm.

Thermometers

A **thermometer measures** exactly how hot or cold something is. This doctor is using a thermometer to measure the **temperature** of the girl's body.

Temperature is measured in **degrees Fahrenheit**, or **°F**. Normal temperature for people is 98.6 °F.

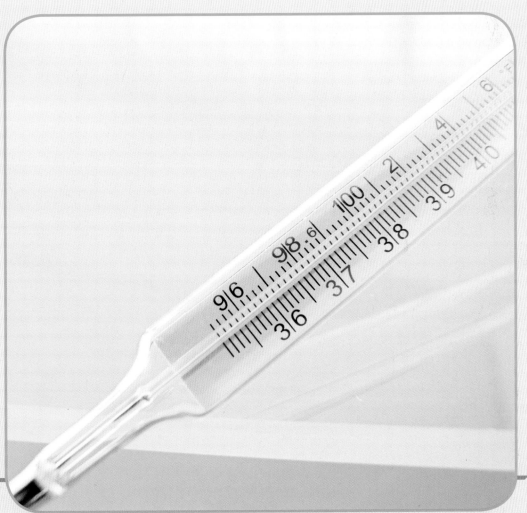

More Thermometers

This **thermometer measures** the **temperature** of the air in a room. It shows 68 **degrees Fahrenheit (°F)**.

This thermometer measures the temperature of the air outside. A temperature of 90 °F is very hot. But 5 °F is very cold.

Keeping Cool

In hot weather we dress to keep ourselves as cool as possible. Many people wear light, loose clothes. These protect them from the sun.

These people live in a very hot place.

Wind can make you feel cooler. This girl
is holding a fan which makes a wind. The
wind cools her down.

Keeping Warm

Hats, gloves, and coats keep cold air out. What special clothes are these children putting on to keep warm? (Answer on page 31.)

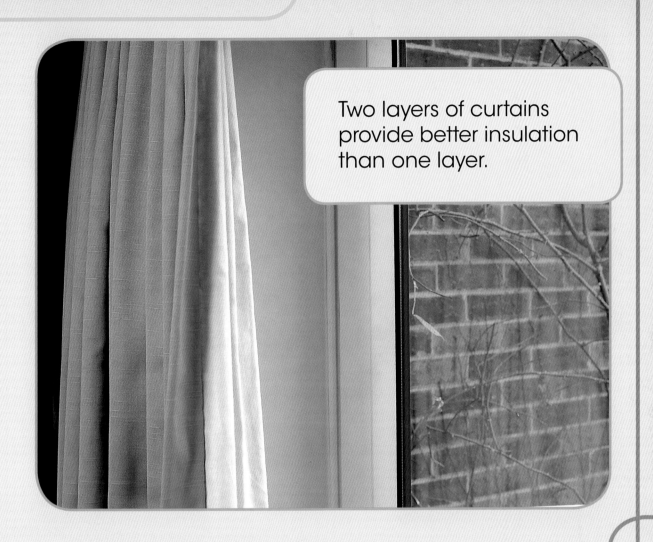

Two layers of curtains provide better insulation than one layer.

Insulation keeps warm air in and cold air out. Windows may have two layers of glass to keep the heat in. Curtains help to **insulate** the house as well.

Cooking

Water is heated to make it boil.

Some food must be cooked to make it safe to eat. When water is heated to 212 **degrees Fahrenheit** it is at its boiling point.

This girl is making a cake. She stirs the **ingredients** which make a runny **liquid** mixture. When the mixture is cooked in a hot oven, it turns **solid**.

Refrigerators

A refrigerator keeps food colder than the air in the room does. The temperature in a refrigerator is just above the **freezing point** of water.

When food is stored in a cold refrigerator, it stays **fresh** for longer.

The bottom of the refrigerator is the coldest part. But if there is a freezer **compartment**, it is even colder. What is stored in the coldest part of this refrigerator? (Answer on page 31.)

Freezing

A freezer keeps food even colder than a refrigerator. The temperature of a freezer is below 32 **degrees Fahrenheit (°F)**, which is the **freezing point** of water.

Ice cubes melt when they are taken out of the freezer and put into warmer drinks.

This boy is putting a tray of water into the freezer. The water will get colder. When it reaches 32 °F, it will turn into **solid** ice cubes.

Melting

This boy is enjoying ice cream. As the cold ice cream becomes warmer, it starts to melt. It changes from **solid** spoonfuls into a runny **liquid**.

Chocolate should not be melted directly in a pan, but in a bowl over hot water.

If you heat chocolate, it will start to melt. When the chocolate cools down, it becomes solid again.

Glossary

compartment small box

degrees Fahrenheit (°F) units of measurement on a thermometer

freezing point temperature at which a liquid becomes a solid

fresh nice to eat, not old

ingredients the different parts of a mixture

insulate stop heat or cold from passing through

insulation a material that keeps heat in and cold out

liquid stuff that can flow, such as water or oil

lukewarm slightly warm

measure find out how big, heavy, hot or cold something is

solid something that has a fixed shape and is not a liquid or a gas

steam tiny droplets of very hot water that float in the air

temperature how hot or cold something is

thermometer tool that measures temperature

Answers

Page 20—The children are putting on coats, hats, scarves, gloves and heavy shoes to keep warm.

Page 25—Vegetables, milk, and juice are stored in the coldest part of the refrigerator.

More Books to Read

Mackill, Mary. *Super Senses: Touching.* Chicago: Heinemann Library, 2006.

Sadler, Wendy. *Science In Your Life—Hot and Cold: Feel It!.* Chicago: Raintree, 2006.

Index